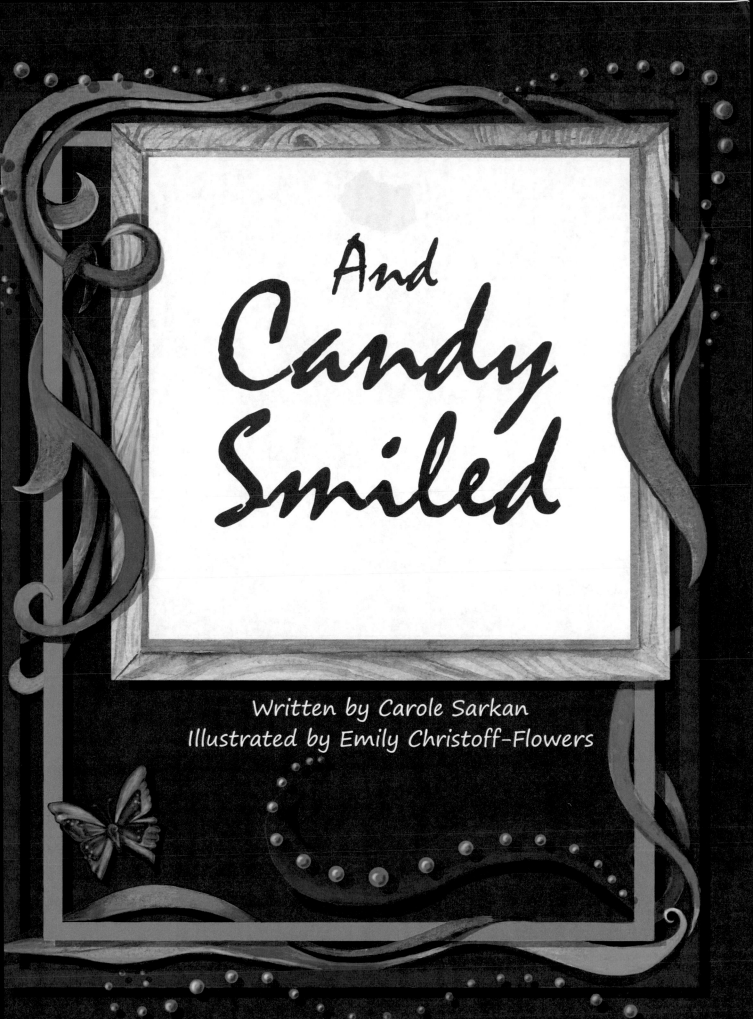

And Candy Smiled

Written by Carole Sarkan
Illustrated by Emily Christoff-Flowers

Balboa Press books may be ordered through booksellers or by contacting:

Balboa Press
A Division of Hay House
1663 Liberty Drive
Bloomington, IN 47403
www.balboapress.com
844-682-1282

ISBN: 978-1-4525-9380-7 (sc)
ISBN: 978-1-9822-6569-4 (hc)
ISBN: 978-1-4525-9381-4 (e)

Print information available on the last page.

Balboa Press rev. date: 04/03/2014

BALBOA.PRESS
A DIVISION OF HAY HOUSE

Dedicated to Brock Bushman
2000-2012

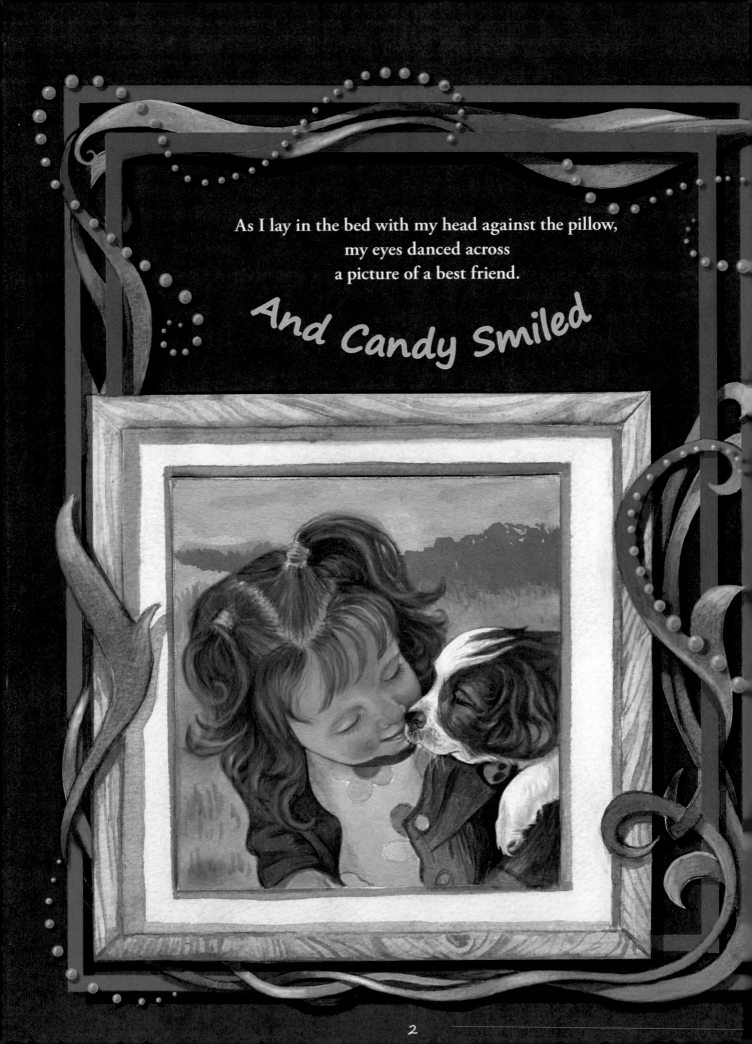

As I lay in the bed with my head against the pillow,
my eyes danced across
a picture of a best friend.

And Candy Smiled

Candy was born in May
as a fat and furry English Springer
slipping and sliding between her sisters and brothers in the yard.
A "C" was marked on her back by her new brown fur.
Candy was her name.
She came home in happy arms that day.

And Candy Smiled

The first day home Candy slipped
and fell to her belly
on the cold kitchen tile.
Emma, Celia and Cassandra
stared and sniffed and growled.
Candy looked at them and cocked her head.

And Candy Smiled

After racing up and down the steep steps,
Candy chewed on soft dog biscuits,
and warm blankets hugged her.
Her eyes closed when her soft fur was brushed.
She dreamed of birds
and squirrels under a warm sun.

And Candy Smiled

Every day Candy raced through the yard,
into the bushes and tall flowers,
past the lilies and trees and fence posts.
She made huge paths
that turned the grass a light brown.
She howled to say hello.

And Candy Smiled

In the glow of fall Candy took us for walks on the towpath.
She rolled and rollicked in the blanket of crisp leaves.
Geese honked her name through the violet skies.

And Candy Smiled

In the winter Candy played games
with the snow.
Cookies were buttery and wrapping paper
was crunchy.
Lights sparkled on the stairway
as she skipped up and down the steep steps.

And Candy Smiled

In the spring, mud puddles turned Candy dark and wet.
Naps were long under the new buds of the trees.
The grass was soft and friendly as she raced after squirrels.

And Candy Smiled

Brownies were too squishy, Toothpaste was too gritty,
Gum was too sticky, Socks were too stringy,
Wash rags were too mushy, but bacon treats made her belly happy.

And Candy Smiled

One day Candy wanted to go to the other side of the fence.
She pushed and pushed on the brick under the old broken gate.
Candy wiggled underneath to the other side of the fence.
Candy ran out to the front yard looking for a place to run.
She wanted to taste the river and
roll in the mowed grass by the canal.

And Candy Smiled

Candy ran down the street to find the river.
She couldn't wait to chase the birds nearby.
So much to see and hear and smell – all for her!
Suddenly something loud and black rumbled toward her.
She stood frozen on the road
and the loud shadow grew closer and larger.
Was it a friend who she could play with?

And Candy Smiled

Then, the black shadow HIT
Candy and she rolled
onto the scratchy stones.
The loud black shadow was gone and
Candy could not move.
After finding her breath,
she gave a weak whimper.
Arms she knew scooped her up
in a flurry of motion….
to "The Place" that had smells
and sounds and faces,
"The Place" she knew she needed.

And Candy Smiled

Then Candy closed her eyes

for a very long time.

Then Candy opened her eyes.
Gentle voices that she did not know were calling her name.
Candy pushed away her soft dog biscuits.
While warm blankets hugged her,
Her eyes closed when her soft fur was brushed.
She dreamed of birds and squirrels under a warm sun.

And Candy Smiled

The next day, Candy's red eyes opened and looked out into the room.
Her tired body shook with warmth when she saw the faces of her family.
They were looking at Candy's three legs instead of four.
"The Place" had to remove her broken leg so Candy could live.
Three legs instead of four, so Candy could live!
Careful arms scooped her up in a flurry of motion to take her back home.

And Candy Smiled

When she returned home,
Candy slipped and fell to her belly
on the cold kitchen tile.
Emma, Celia and Cassandra
stared and sniffed and growled.
Candy looked at them and cocked her head.

And Candy Smiled

Candy hobbled and limped and licked
where her leg should have been.
From the door, she watched the spring puddles.
The buds on the trees missed Candy's long naps.
She drank lots of water
and didn't touch her dog biscuits.
Walking was tripping and limping on three legs,
a new experience.
She was home, though and that was enough.

And Candy Smiled

As Candy lay in her warm bed on a wet spring morning,
raindrops filled puddles in the alley.
Squirrels chattered her name.
The buds wanted Candy to take naps with them.
Birds sang melodies calling her to play.
The breeze blown grasses needed Candy
to make her path in the yard again.

And Candy Smiled

The next day, Candy hobbled to the door.
She heard the backyard calling her name!
And then she knew what she needed to do.

And Candy Smiled

She decided to:
race through the yard,
into the bushes and tall flowers,
past the lilies and trees and fence posts ---
She made huge paths
that turned the grass a light brown.
She howled to say hello.

And Candy Smiled

Candy learned to walk on three legs instead of four.
Three legs instead of four----
so Candy could live!
She ran up and down the steep steps.
She visited children and old folks.
She watched softball at the busy ballparks.

And Candy Smiled

After racing up and down the steep steps,
Candy chewed on soft dog biscuits
while warm blankets hugged her.
Her eyes closed when her soft fur was brushed.
She dreamed of birds and squirrels under a warm sun.

And Candy Smiled

As I lay in the bed with my head against the pillow,
my eyes danced across
a picture of my best friend.

And Candy Smiled

About the Author

Carole Sarkan is a school teacher who has always had a passion for writing, music, history, and art. She decided to put these interests together when she finished college and become a teacher. Since the age of six she has always wanted to write children's books. Now her dream is happening. With the partnership of Emily Christoff-Flowers as her illustrator, they are embarking on a new adventure about Carole's English springer spaniel dog, Candy. Carole comes from a family of artists. Her grandparents were song writers, her mother and father were musicians who loved writing eloquent letters, and her brother Jim Grabill is a prolific poet and teacher in Portland, Oregon. Carole is originally from Bowling Green, Ohio and currently lives in Grand Rapids, Ohio. She teaches 4th grade writing, reading and history at Kenwood Elementary in Bowling Green, Ohio.

About the Artist

Emily Christoff-Flowers has always had a fascination with drawing people, animals and nature since she was a little girl growing up in the farmlands of Ohio. Her parents supported her love of painting and encouraged her to pursue art as a career. She earned her Bachelors of Fine Arts degree from Bowling Green State University in Bowling Green, Ohio in 1987. She has supported herself for the past 27 years by selling her work. She currently teaches art, works as a portrait artist by painting people as well as pets in Williamsburg, Virginia. You may see more examples of her work at

www.EmilyChristoff.com

Printed in the United States
by Baker & Taylor Publisher Services